## DATE

## LOCATION

## GPS

## WEATHER CONDITIONS

## SET-UP

MACHINE & EQUIPMENT

USED SETTINGS

## SKETCHES

D0967195

## LIST OF ITEMS

| ITEM FOUND | MAIN MATERIAL | WEIGHT & SIZE | VALUE |
|------------|---------------|---------------|-------|
|            |               |               |       |
|            |               |               |       |
|            |               |               |       |
|            |               |               |       |
|            |               |               |       |
|            |               |               |       |
|            |               |               |       |
|            |               |               |       |
|            |               |               |       |
|            |               |               |       |
|            |               |               |       |

## DATE

## LOCATION

## GPS

## WEATHER CONDITIONS

## SET-UP

**MACHINE & EQUIPMENT**

-
-

**USED SETTINGS**

## SKETCHES

## LIST OF ITEMS

| ITEM FOUND | MAIN MATERIAL | WEIGHT & SIZE | VALUE |
| --- | --- | --- | --- |
| | | | |
| | | | |
| | | | |
| | | | |
| | | | |
| | | | |
| | | | |
| | | | |
| | | | |
| | | | |

| DATE | WEATHER CONDITIONS |
|---|---|

| DATE |
|---|
| LOCATION |
| GPS |

## WEATHER CONDITIONS

## SET-UP

MACHINE & EQUIPMENT

- 
- 

USED SETTINGS

## SKETCHES

## LIST OF ITEMS

| ITEM FOUND | MAIN MATERIAL | WEIGHT & SIZE | VALUE |
|---|---|---|---|
| | | | |
| | | | |
| | | | |
| | | | |
| | | | |
| | | | |
| | | | |
| | | | |
| | | | |
| | | | |

## DATE

## LOCATION

## GPS

## WEATHER CONDITIONS

## SET-UP

### MACHINE & EQUIPMENT

- 
- 

### USED SETTINGS

## SKETCHES

## LIST OF ITEMS

| ITEM FOUND | MAIN MATERIAL | WEIGHT & SIZE | VALUE |
|---|---|---|---|
| | | | |
| | | | |
| | | | |
| | | | |
| | | | |
| | | | |
| | | | |
| | | | |
| | | | |
| | | | |

## DATE

## LOCATION

## GPS

## WEATHER CONDITIONS

☀ ⛅ 🌧 ⛈ ❄

☐ ☐ ☐ ☐ ☐

## SET-UP

### MACHINE & EQUIPMENT

### USED SETTINGS

## SKETCHES

## LIST OF ITEMS

| ITEM FOUND | MAIN MATERIAL | WEIGHT & SIZE | VALUE |
|---|---|---|---|
| | | | |
| | | | |
| | | | |
| | | | |
| | | | |
| | | | |
| | | | |
| | | | |
| | | | |
| | | | |

## DATE

## LOCATION

## GPS

## WEATHER CONDITIONS

## SET-UP

### MACHINE & EQUIPMENT

- 
- 

### USED SETTINGS

## SKETCHES

## LIST OF ITEMS

| ITEM FOUND | MAIN MATERIAL | WEIGHT & SIZE | VALUE |
|------------|---------------|---------------|-------|
|            |               |               |       |
|            |               |               |       |
|            |               |               |       |
|            |               |               |       |
|            |               |               |       |
|            |               |               |       |
|            |               |               |       |
|            |               |               |       |
|            |               |               |       |
|            |               |               |       |

| 📅 DATE | | **WEATHER CONDITIONS** | | | | | |
|---|---|---|---|---|---|---|---|
| 📍 LOCATION | | 🌡️ ___ | ☀️ | ⛅ | 🌧️ | ⛈️ | ❄️ |
| 🧭 GPS | | 🚩 ___ | ☐ | ☐ | ☐ | ☐ | ☐ |

## SET-UP

📱 MACHINE & EQUIPMENT

•

•

🎚️ USED SETTINGS

## SKETCHES

## LIST OF ITEMS

| 💎 ITEM FOUND | 📑 MAIN MATERIAL | ⚖️ WEIGHT & SIZE | 🏷️ VALUE |
|---|---|---|---|
| | | | |
| | | | |
| | | | |
| | | | |
| | | | |
| | | | |
| | | | |
| | | | |
| | | | |
| | | | |

| 📅 DATE | |
|---|---|
| 📍 LOCATION | |
| 🧭 GPS | |

## WEATHER CONDITIONS

🌡 ___  ☀️ ⛅ 🌧 ⛈ ❄️

🚩 ___  ☐ ☐ ☐ ☐ ☐

## SET-UP

| 📟 MACHINE & EQUIPMENT |
|---|
| • |
| • |
| 🎚 USED SETTINGS |
| |
| |
| |

## SKETCHES

## LIST OF ITEMS

| 💎 ITEM FOUND | 📚 MAIN MATERIAL | ⚖️ WEIGHT & SIZE | 🏷 VALUE |
|---|---|---|---|
| | | | |
| | | | |
| | | | |
| | | | |
| | | | |
| | | | |
| | | | |
| | | | |
| | | | |
| | | | |

| 📅 DATE | **WEATHER CONDITIONS** |
|---|---|

| 📅 **DATE** |
|---|
| 📍 **LOCATION** |
| 🧭 **GPS** |

**WEATHER CONDITIONS**

🌡 ____ ☀️ ⛅ 🌧 ⛈ ❄️

🚩 ____ ☐ ☐ ☐ ☐ ☐

| **SET-UP** | **SKETCHES** |
|---|---|

| **SET-UP** |
|---|
| 📱 MACHINE & EQUIPMENT |
| • |
| • |
| 🎚 USED SETTINGS |
| |
| |
| |

**SKETCHES**

## LIST OF ITEMS

| 💎 ITEM FOUND | 🗂 MAIN MATERIAL | ⚖️ WEIGHT & SIZE | 🏷 VALUE |
|---|---|---|---|
| | | | |
| | | | |
| | | | |
| | | | |
| | | | |
| | | | |
| | | | |
| | | | |
| | | | |
| | | | |

| 📅 DATE | |
|---|---|
| 📍 LOCATION | |
| 🧭 GPS | |

## WEATHER CONDITIONS

🌡️ ——  ☀️ ⛅ 🌧️ ⛈️ ❄️

🚩 ——  ☐ ☐ ☐ ☐ ☐

## SET-UP

📟 MACHINE & EQUIPMENT

- •
- •

🎚️ USED SETTINGS

## SKETCHES

## LIST OF ITEMS

| 💎 ITEM FOUND | 📑 MAIN MATERIAL | ⚖️ WEIGHT & SIZE | 🏷️ VALUE |
|---|---|---|---|
| | | | |
| | | | |
| | | | |
| | | | |
| | | | |
| | | | |
| | | | |
| | | | |
| | | | |
| | | | |

**DATE**

**LOCATION**

**GPS**

## WEATHER CONDITIONS

## SET-UP

MACHINE & EQUIPMENT

USED SETTINGS

## SKETCHES

## LIST OF ITEMS

| ITEM FOUND | MAIN MATERIAL | WEIGHT & SIZE | VALUE |
|---|---|---|---|
| | | | |
| | | | |
| | | | |
| | | | |
| | | | |
| | | | |
| | | | |
| | | | |
| | | | |
| | | | |

| 📅 **DATE** | **WEATHER CONDITIONS** |
|---|---|

| 📅 **DATE** |
|---|
| 📍 **LOCATION** |
| 🧭 **GPS** |

**WEATHER CONDITIONS**

🌡 ___ ☀ ⛅ ☁ 🌧 ❄

🚩 ___ ☐ ☐ ☐ ☐ ☐

## SET-UP

| 📱 MACHINE & EQUIPMENT |
|---|
| • |
| • |
| ⚙ USED SETTINGS |
| |
| |
| |

## SKETCHES

## LIST OF ITEMS

| 💎 ITEM FOUND | 🍥 MAIN MATERIAL | ⚖ WEIGHT & SIZE | 🏷 VALUE |
|---|---|---|---|
| | | | |
| | | | |
| | | | |
| | | | |
| | | | |
| | | | |
| | | | |
| | | | |
| | | | |
| | | | |

| DATE | | WEATHER CONDITIONS | | | | | |
|------|--|--------------------|--|--|--|--|--|

**DATE**

**LOCATION**

**GPS**

## WEATHER CONDITIONS

🌡 ——  ☀ ⛅ 🌧 ⛈ ❄

🚩 ——  ☐ ☐ ☐ ☐ ☐

## SET-UP

**MACHINE & EQUIPMENT**

•

•

**USED SETTINGS**

## SKETCHES

## LIST OF ITEMS

| ITEM FOUND | MAIN MATERIAL | WEIGHT & SIZE | VALUE |
|------------|---------------|---------------|-------|
| | | | |
| | | | |
| | | | |
| | | | |
| | | | |
| | | | |
| | | | |
| | | | |
| | | | |
| | | | |
| | | | |

## DATE

## LOCATION

## GPS

## WEATHER CONDITIONS

## SET-UP

**MACHINE & EQUIPMENT**

·

·

**USED SETTINGS**

## SKETCHES

## LIST OF ITEMS

| ITEM FOUND | MAIN MATERIAL | WEIGHT & SIZE | VALUE |
|---|---|---|---|
| | | | |
| | | | |
| | | | |
| | | | |
| | | | |
| | | | |
| | | | |
| | | | |
| | | | |
| | | | |

| DATE | WEATHER CONDITIONS |
|---|---|

**DATE**

**LOCATION**

**GPS**

## WEATHER CONDITIONS

## SET-UP

**MACHINE & EQUIPMENT**

·

·

**USED SETTINGS**

## SKETCHES

## LIST OF ITEMS

| ITEM FOUND | MAIN MATERIAL | WEIGHT & SIZE | VALUE |
|---|---|---|---|
| | | | |
| | | | |
| | | | |
| | | | |
| | | | |
| | | | |
| | | | |
| | | | |
| | | | |
| | | | |
| | | | |

## DATE

## LOCATION

## GPS

## WEATHER CONDITIONS

## SET-UP

**MACHINE & EQUIPMENT**

- 
- 

**USED SETTINGS**

## SKETCHES

## LIST OF ITEMS

| ITEM FOUND | MAIN MATERIAL | WEIGHT & SIZE | VALUE |
|---|---|---|---|
| | | | |
| | | | |
| | | | |
| | | | |
| | | | |
| | | | |
| | | | |
| | | | |
| | | | |
| | | | |

## DATE

## LOCATION

## GPS

## WEATHER CONDITIONS

## SET-UP

MACHINE & EQUIPMENT

USED SETTINGS

## SKETCHES

## LIST OF ITEMS

| ITEM FOUND | MAIN MATERIAL | WEIGHT & SIZE | VALUE |
|---|---|---|---|
| | | | |
| | | | |
| | | | |
| | | | |
| | | | |
| | | | |
| | | | |
| | | | |
| | | | |
| | | | |
| | | | |

| 📅 DATE | |
|---|---|
| 📍 LOCATION | |
| 🧭 GPS | |

## WEATHER CONDITIONS

🌡️ ___ ☀️ ⛅ 🌧️ ⛈️ ❄️

🌬️ ___ ☐ ☐ ☐ ☐ ☐

## SET-UP

📱 MACHINE & EQUIPMENT

- 
- 

🎛️ USED SETTINGS

## SKETCHES

## LIST OF ITEMS

| 💎 ITEM FOUND | 📑 MAIN MATERIAL | ⚖️ WEIGHT & SIZE | 🏷️ VALUE |
|---|---|---|---|
| | | | |
| | | | |
| | | | |
| | | | |
| | | | |
| | | | |
| | | | |
| | | | |
| | | | |
| | | | |

## DATE

## LOCATION

## GPS

## WEATHER CONDITIONS

## SET-UP

**MACHINE & EQUIPMENT**

- 
- 

**USED SETTINGS**

## SKETCHES

## LIST OF ITEMS

| ITEM FOUND | MAIN MATERIAL | WEIGHT & SIZE | VALUE |
| --- | --- | --- | --- |
|  |  |  |  |
|  |  |  |  |
|  |  |  |  |
|  |  |  |  |
|  |  |  |  |
|  |  |  |  |
|  |  |  |  |
|  |  |  |  |
|  |  |  |  |
|  |  |  |  |

## DATE

## LOCATION

## GPS

## WEATHER CONDITIONS

## SET-UP

### MACHINE & EQUIPMENT

- 
- 

### USED SETTINGS

## SKETCHES

## LIST OF ITEMS

| ITEM FOUND | MAIN MATERIAL | WEIGHT & SIZE | VALUE |
|---|---|---|---|
|  |  |  |  |
|  |  |  |  |
|  |  |  |  |
|  |  |  |  |
|  |  |  |  |
|  |  |  |  |
|  |  |  |  |
|  |  |  |  |
|  |  |  |  |
|  |  |  |  |

| DATE | WEATHER CONDITIONS |
|---|---|

**DATE**

**LOCATION**

**GPS**

## WEATHER CONDITIONS

## SET-UP

**MACHINE & EQUIPMENT**

- 
- 

**USED SETTINGS**

## SKETCHES

## LIST OF ITEMS

| ITEM FOUND | MAIN MATERIAL | WEIGHT & SIZE | VALUE |
|---|---|---|---|
|  |  |  |  |
|  |  |  |  |
|  |  |  |  |
|  |  |  |  |
|  |  |  |  |
|  |  |  |  |
|  |  |  |  |
|  |  |  |  |
|  |  |  |  |
|  |  |  |  |
|  |  |  |  |
|  |  |  |  |

## DATE

## LOCATION

## GPS

## WEATHER CONDITIONS

## SET-UP

**MACHINE & EQUIPMENT**

•

•

**USED SETTINGS**

## SKETCHES

## LIST OF ITEMS

| ITEM FOUND | MAIN MATERIAL | WEIGHT & SIZE | VALUE |
|---|---|---|---|
| | | | |
| | | | |
| | | | |
| | | | |
| | | | |
| | | | |
| | | | |
| | | | |
| | | | |
| | | | |

## DATE

## LOCATION

## GPS

## WEATHER CONDITIONS

## SET-UP

MACHINE & EQUIPMENT

USED SETTINGS

## SKETCHES

## LIST OF ITEMS

| ITEM FOUND | MAIN MATERIAL | WEIGHT & SIZE | VALUE |
|---|---|---|---|
| | | | |
| | | | |
| | | | |
| | | | |
| | | | |
| | | | |
| | | | |
| | | | |
| | | | |
| | | | |

## DATE

## LOCATION

## GPS

## WEATHER CONDITIONS

## SET-UP

### MACHINE & EQUIPMENT

-

-

### USED SETTINGS

## SKETCHES

## LIST OF ITEMS

| ITEM FOUND | MAIN MATERIAL | WEIGHT & SIZE | VALUE |
|---|---|---|---|
| | | | |
| | | | |
| | | | |
| | | | |
| | | | |
| | | | |
| | | | |
| | | | |
| | | | |
| | | | |

## DATE

## LOCATION

## GPS

## WEATHER CONDITIONS

## SET-UP

**MACHINE & EQUIPMENT**

- 

- 

**USED SETTINGS**

## SKETCHES

## LIST OF ITEMS

| ITEM FOUND | MAIN MATERIAL | WEIGHT & SIZE | VALUE |
|---|---|---|---|
|  |  |  |  |
|  |  |  |  |
|  |  |  |  |
|  |  |  |  |
|  |  |  |  |
|  |  |  |  |
|  |  |  |  |
|  |  |  |  |
|  |  |  |  |
|  |  |  |  |

| DATE | |
|---|---|
| LOCATION | |
| GPS | |

## WEATHER CONDITIONS

## SET-UP

MACHINE & EQUIPMENT

- 
- 

USED SETTINGS

## SKETCHES

## LIST OF ITEMS

| ITEM FOUND | MAIN MATERIAL | WEIGHT & SIZE | VALUE |
|---|---|---|---|
| | | | |
| | | | |
| | | | |
| | | | |
| | | | |
| | | | |
| | | | |
| | | | |
| | | | |
| | | | |

## DATE

## LOCATION

## GPS

## WEATHER CONDITIONS

## SET-UP

MACHINE & EQUIPMENT

- 
- 

USED SETTINGS

## SKETCHES

## LIST OF ITEMS

| ITEM FOUND | MAIN MATERIAL | WEIGHT & SIZE | VALUE |
|------------|---------------|---------------|-------|
|  |  |  |  |
|  |  |  |  |
|  |  |  |  |
|  |  |  |  |
|  |  |  |  |
|  |  |  |  |
|  |  |  |  |
|  |  |  |  |
|  |  |  |  |
|  |  |  |  |
|  |  |  |  |

| 📅 DATE | | **WEATHER CONDITIONS** | | | | | |
|---|---|---|---|---|---|---|---|
| 📍 LOCATION | | 🌡️ ___ | ☀️ | ⛅ | ☁️ | 🌧️ | ❄️ |
| 🧭 GPS | | 🚩 ___ | ☐ | ☐ | ☐ | ☐ | ☐ |

## SET-UP

🎛️ MACHINE & EQUIPMENT

•

•

🎚️ USED SETTINGS

## SKETCHES

## LIST OF ITEMS

| 💎 ITEM FOUND | 🗇 MAIN MATERIAL | ⚖️ WEIGHT & SIZE | 🏷️ VALUE |
|---|---|---|---|
| | | | |
| | | | |
| | | | |
| | | | |
| | | | |
| | | | |
| | | | |
| | | | |
| | | | |
| | | | |

**DATE** _____

**LOCATION** _____

**GPS** _____

## WEATHER CONDITIONS

🌡️ _____  ☀️ ⛅ 🌧️ ⛈️ ❄️

🚩 _____  ☐ ☐ ☐ ☐ ☐

## SET-UP

**MACHINE & EQUIPMENT**
_____
_____
_____

**USED SETTINGS**
_____
_____
_____

## SKETCHES

## LIST OF ITEMS

| ITEM FOUND | MAIN MATERIAL | WEIGHT & SIZE | VALUE |
|---|---|---|---|
| | | | |
| | | | |
| | | | |
| | | | |
| | | | |
| | | | |
| | | | |
| | | | |
| | | | |
| | | | |

| DATE |
|---|
| LOCATION |
| GPS |

## WEATHER CONDITIONS

🌡 ___   ☀ ⛅ ☁ ⛈ ❄

🚩 ___   ☐ ☐ ☐ ☐ ☐

## SET-UP

MACHINE & EQUIPMENT

•

•

USED SETTINGS

## SKETCHES

## LIST OF ITEMS

| 💎 ITEM FOUND | 📚 MAIN MATERIAL | ⚖ WEIGHT & SIZE | 🏷 VALUE |
|---|---|---|---|
|  |  |  |  |
|  |  |  |  |
|  |  |  |  |
|  |  |  |  |
|  |  |  |  |
|  |  |  |  |
|  |  |  |  |
|  |  |  |  |
|  |  |  |  |
|  |  |  |  |

## DATE

## LOCATION

## GPS

## WEATHER CONDITIONS

## SET-UP

### MACHINE & EQUIPMENT

- 
- 

### USED SETTINGS

## SKETCHES

## LIST OF ITEMS

| ITEM FOUND | MAIN MATERIAL | WEIGHT & SIZE | VALUE |
|---|---|---|---|
| | | | |
| | | | |
| | | | |
| | | | |
| | | | |
| | | | |
| | | | |
| | | | |
| | | | |
| | | | |
| | | | |

| 📅 DATE | |
|---|---|
| 📍 LOCATION | |
| 🧭 GPS | |

## WEATHER CONDITIONS

🌡 ——  ☀️ ⛅ 🌧 ⛈ ❄️

🎐 ——  ☐ ☐ ☐ ☐ ☐

## SET-UP

| 📱 MACHINE & EQUIPMENT |
|---|
| • |
| • |
| 🎚 USED SETTINGS |
| |
| |
| |

## SKETCHES

## LIST OF ITEMS

| 💎 ITEM FOUND | 🔶 MAIN MATERIAL | ⚖️ WEIGHT & SIZE | 🏷 VALUE |
|---|---|---|---|
| | | | |
| | | | |
| | | | |
| | | | |
| | | | |
| | | | |
| | | | |
| | | | |
| | | | |
| | | | |

## DATE

## LOCATION

## GPS

## WEATHER CONDITIONS

## SET-UP

### MACHINE & EQUIPMENT

-
-

### USED SETTINGS

## SKETCHES

## LIST OF ITEMS

| ITEM FOUND | MAIN MATERIAL | WEIGHT & SIZE | VALUE |
|---|---|---|---|
|  |  |  |  |
|  |  |  |  |
|  |  |  |  |
|  |  |  |  |
|  |  |  |  |
|  |  |  |  |
|  |  |  |  |
|  |  |  |  |
|  |  |  |  |
|  |  |  |  |
|  |  |  |  |

| DATE | |
|------|--|
| LOCATION | |
| GPS | |

## WEATHER CONDITIONS

| 🌡 ___ | ☀ | ⛅ | 🌧 | ⛈ | ❄ |
|--------|---|----|----|----|----|
| 🚩 ___ | ☐ | ☐ | ☐ | ☐ | ☐ |

## SET-UP

| MACHINE & EQUIPMENT |
|---------------------|
| • |
| • |
| USED SETTINGS |
| |
| |
| |

## SKETCHES

## LIST OF ITEMS

| ITEM FOUND | MAIN MATERIAL | WEIGHT & SIZE | VALUE |
|------------|---------------|---------------|-------|
| | | | |
| | | | |
| | | | |
| | | | |
| | | | |
| | | | |
| | | | |
| | | | |
| | | | |
| | | | |

| DATE | | WEATHER CONDITIONS |
|---|---|---|

DATE

LOCATION

GPS

## WEATHER CONDITIONS

## SET-UP

MACHINE & EQUIPMENT

USED SETTINGS

## SKETCHES

## LIST OF ITEMS

| ITEM FOUND | MAIN MATERIAL | WEIGHT & SIZE | VALUE |
|---|---|---|---|
| | | | |
| | | | |
| | | | |
| | | | |
| | | | |
| | | | |
| | | | |
| | | | |
| | | | |
| | | | |
| | | | |

| 📅 DATE | |
|---|---|
| 📍 LOCATION | |
| 🧭 GPS | |

## WEATHER CONDITIONS

🌡 ___ ☀ ⛅ 🌧 🌧 ❄

🚩 ___ ☐ ☐ ☐ ☐ ☐

## SET-UP

| 📱 MACHINE & EQUIPMENT |
|---|
| • |
| • |
| ⚙ USED SETTINGS |
| |
| |
| |

## SKETCHES

## LIST OF ITEMS

| 💎 ITEM FOUND | 📚 MAIN MATERIAL | ⚖ WEIGHT & SIZE | 🏷 VALUE |
|---|---|---|---|
| | | | |
| | | | |
| | | | |
| | | | |
| | | | |
| | | | |
| | | | |
| | | | |
| | | | |
| | | | |

# DATE

# LOCATION

# GPS

## WEATHER CONDITIONS

## SET-UP

MACHINE & EQUIPMENT

- 
- 

USED SETTINGS

## SKETCHES

## LIST OF ITEMS

| ITEM FOUND | MAIN MATERIAL | WEIGHT & SIZE | VALUE |
|---|---|---|---|
|  |  |  |  |
|  |  |  |  |
|  |  |  |  |
|  |  |  |  |
|  |  |  |  |
|  |  |  |  |
|  |  |  |  |
|  |  |  |  |
|  |  |  |  |
|  |  |  |  |

| 📅 DATE | | **WEATHER CONDITIONS** | | | | | |
|---|---|---|---|---|---|---|---|
| 📍 LOCATION | | 🌡 ___ | ☀ | ⛅ | 🌧 | ⛈ | ❄ |
| 🧭 GPS | | 🚩 ___ | ☐ | ☐ | ☐ | ☐ | ☐ |

## SET-UP

| 📟 MACHINE & EQUIPMENT |
|---|
| • |
| • |
| 🎛 USED SETTINGS |
| |
| |
| |

## SKETCHES

## LIST OF ITEMS

| 💎 ITEM FOUND | 📑 MAIN MATERIAL | ⚖ WEIGHT & SIZE | 🏷 VALUE |
|---|---|---|---|
| | | | |
| | | | |
| | | | |
| | | | |
| | | | |
| | | | |
| | | | |
| | | | |
| | | | |
| | | | |

| DATE | WEATHER CONDITIONS |
|---|---|

**DATE**

**LOCATION**

**GPS**

## WEATHER CONDITIONS

## SET-UP

**MACHINE & EQUIPMENT**

•

•

**USED SETTINGS**

## SKETCHES

## LIST OF ITEMS

| ITEM FOUND | MAIN MATERIAL | WEIGHT & SIZE | VALUE |
|---|---|---|---|
| | | | |
| | | | |
| | | | |
| | | | |
| | | | |
| | | | |
| | | | |
| | | | |
| | | | |
| | | | |
| | | | |
| | | | |

## DATE

## LOCATION

## GPS

## WEATHER CONDITIONS

## SET-UP

**MACHINE & EQUIPMENT**

- 
- 

**USED SETTINGS**

## SKETCHES

## LIST OF ITEMS

| ITEM FOUND | MAIN MATERIAL | WEIGHT & SIZE | VALUE |
|---|---|---|---|
|  |  |  |  |
|  |  |  |  |
|  |  |  |  |
|  |  |  |  |
|  |  |  |  |
|  |  |  |  |
|  |  |  |  |
|  |  |  |  |
|  |  |  |  |
|  |  |  |  |

## DATE

## LOCATION

## GPS

## WEATHER CONDITIONS

## SET-UP

**MACHINE & EQUIPMENT**

**USED SETTINGS**

## SKETCHES

## LIST OF ITEMS

| ITEM FOUND | MAIN MATERIAL | WEIGHT & SIZE | VALUE |
|---|---|---|---|
| | | | |
| | | | |
| | | | |
| | | | |
| | | | |
| | | | |
| | | | |
| | | | |
| | | | |
| | | | |

| 📅 **DATE** | |
|---|---|
| 📍 **LOCATION** | |
| 🧭 **GPS** | |

## WEATHER CONDITIONS

🌡 ___ ☀ ⛅ 🌧 ⛈ ❄

🚩 ___ ☐ ☐ ☐ ☐ ☐

## SET-UP

📱 MACHINE & EQUIPMENT

• 

• 

🎚 USED SETTINGS

## SKETCHES

## LIST OF ITEMS

| 💎 ITEM FOUND | 🗄 MAIN MATERIAL | ⚖ WEIGHT & SIZE | 🏷 VALUE |
|---|---|---|---|
| | | | |
| | | | |
| | | | |
| | | | |
| | | | |
| | | | |
| | | | |
| | | | |
| | | | |
| | | | |

## DATE

## LOCATION

## GPS

## WEATHER CONDITIONS

## SET-UP

### MACHINE & EQUIPMENT

- 

- 

### USED SETTINGS

## SKETCHES

## LIST OF ITEMS

| ITEM FOUND | MAIN MATERIAL | WEIGHT & SIZE | VALUE |
|---|---|---|---|
| | | | |
| | | | |
| | | | |
| | | | |
| | | | |
| | | | |
| | | | |
| | | | |
| | | | |
| | | | |

## DATE

## LOCATION

## GPS

## WEATHER CONDITIONS

## SET-UP

**MACHINE & EQUIPMENT**

- •
- •

**USED SETTINGS**

## SKETCHES

## LIST OF ITEMS

| ITEM FOUND | MAIN MATERIAL | WEIGHT & SIZE | VALUE |
|---|---|---|---|
| | | | |
| | | | |
| | | | |
| | | | |
| | | | |
| | | | |
| | | | |
| | | | |
| | | | |
| | | | |

## DATE

## LOCATION

## GPS

## WEATHER CONDITIONS

## SET-UP

**MACHINE & EQUIPMENT**

- 
- 

**USED SETTINGS**

## SKETCHES

## LIST OF ITEMS

| ITEM FOUND | MAIN MATERIAL | WEIGHT & SIZE | VALUE |
|---|---|---|---|
|  |  |  |  |
|  |  |  |  |
|  |  |  |  |
|  |  |  |  |
|  |  |  |  |
|  |  |  |  |
|  |  |  |  |
|  |  |  |  |
|  |  |  |  |
|  |  |  |  |

## DATE

## LOCATION

## GPS

## WEATHER CONDITIONS

## SET-UP

**MACHINE & EQUIPMENT**

-

-

**USED SETTINGS**

## SKETCHES

## LIST OF ITEMS

| ITEM FOUND | MAIN MATERIAL | WEIGHT & SIZE | VALUE |
|---|---|---|---|
| | | | |
| | | | |
| | | | |
| | | | |
| | | | |
| | | | |
| | | | |
| | | | |
| | | | |
| | | | |

## DATE

## LOCATION

## GPS

## WEATHER CONDITIONS

## SET-UP

### MACHINE & EQUIPMENT

### USED SETTINGS

## SKETCHES

## LIST OF ITEMS

| ITEM FOUND | MAIN MATERIAL | WEIGHT & SIZE | VALUE |
|------------|---------------|---------------|-------|
|            |               |               |       |
|            |               |               |       |
|            |               |               |       |
|            |               |               |       |
|            |               |               |       |
|            |               |               |       |
|            |               |               |       |
|            |               |               |       |
|            |               |               |       |
|            |               |               |       |
|            |               |               |       |

| 📅 DATE | **WEATHER CONDITIONS** |
| 📍 LOCATION | 🌡 ___  ☀ 🌤 ☁ 🌧 ❄ |
| 🧭 GPS | 🚩 ___  ☐ ☐ ☐ ☐ ☐ |

## SET-UP

📱 MACHINE & EQUIPMENT

- •
- •

⚙ USED SETTINGS

## SKETCHES

## LIST OF ITEMS

| 💎 ITEM FOUND | 🗂 MAIN MATERIAL | ⚖ WEIGHT & SIZE | 🏷 VALUE |
|---|---|---|---|
| | | | |
| | | | |
| | | | |
| | | | |
| | | | |
| | | | |
| | | | |
| | | | |
| | | | |
| | | | |

## DATE

## LOCATION

## GPS

## WEATHER CONDITIONS

## SET-UP

MACHINE & EQUIPMENT

- 

- 

USED SETTINGS

## SKETCHES

## LIST OF ITEMS

| ITEM FOUND | MAIN MATERIAL | WEIGHT & SIZE | VALUE |
|---|---|---|---|
| | | | |
| | | | |
| | | | |
| | | | |
| | | | |
| | | | |
| | | | |
| | | | |
| | | | |
| | | | |

| DATE | WEATHER CONDITIONS |

## DATE

## LOCATION

## GPS

## WEATHER CONDITIONS

## SET-UP

MACHINE & EQUIPMENT

- 
- 

USED SETTINGS

## SKETCHES

## LIST OF ITEMS

| ITEM FOUND | MAIN MATERIAL | WEIGHT & SIZE | VALUE |
|---|---|---|---|
| | | | |
| | | | |
| | | | |
| | | | |
| | | | |
| | | | |
| | | | |
| | | | |
| | | | |
| | | | |

## DATE

## LOCATION

## GPS

## WEATHER CONDITIONS

## SET-UP

**MACHINE & EQUIPMENT**

·

·

**USED SETTINGS**

## SKETCHES

## LIST OF ITEMS

| ITEM FOUND | MAIN MATERIAL | WEIGHT & SIZE | VALUE |
|---|---|---|---|
| | | | |
| | | | |
| | | | |
| | | | |
| | | | |
| | | | |
| | | | |
| | | | |
| | | | |
| | | | |

| 📅 DATE | WEATHER CONDITIONS |
|---------|--------------------|

| 📅 DATE |
|---------|
| 📍 LOCATION |
| 🧭 GPS |

## WEATHER CONDITIONS

🌡 ____   ☀️  ⛅  🌧  ⛈  ❄️

🚩 ____   ☐  ☐  ☐  ☐  ☐

## SET-UP

| 📱 MACHINE & EQUIPMENT |
|------------------------|
| • |
| • |
| 🎚 USED SETTINGS |
| |
| |
| |

## SKETCHES

## LIST OF ITEMS

| 💎 ITEM FOUND | 🍥 MAIN MATERIAL | ⚖️ WEIGHT & SIZE | 🏷 VALUE |
|---------------|------------------|------------------|----------|
| | | | |
| | | | |
| | | | |
| | | | |
| | | | |
| | | | |
| | | | |
| | | | |
| | | | |
| | | | |

## DATE

## LOCATION

## GPS

## WEATHER CONDITIONS

## SET-UP

MACHINE & EQUIPMENT

USED SETTINGS

## SKETCHES

## LIST OF ITEMS

| ITEM FOUND | MAIN MATERIAL | WEIGHT & SIZE | VALUE |
|---|---|---|---|
|  |  |  |  |
|  |  |  |  |
|  |  |  |  |
|  |  |  |  |
|  |  |  |  |
|  |  |  |  |
|  |  |  |  |
|  |  |  |  |
|  |  |  |  |
|  |  |  |  |
|  |  |  |  |

| 🗓 DATE |
| --- |
| 📍 LOCATION |
| 🧭 GPS |

## WEATHER CONDITIONS

🌡 ___  ☀️ ⛅ 🌧 ⛈ ❄️

🚩 ___  ☐ ☐ ☐ ☐ ☐

## SET-UP

📱 MACHINE & EQUIPMENT

• 

• 

⚙️ USED SETTINGS

## SKETCHES

## LIST OF ITEMS

| 💎 ITEM FOUND | 📑 MAIN MATERIAL | ⚖️ WEIGHT & SIZE | 🏷 VALUE |
| --- | --- | --- | --- |
|  |  |  |  |
|  |  |  |  |
|  |  |  |  |
|  |  |  |  |
|  |  |  |  |
|  |  |  |  |
|  |  |  |  |
|  |  |  |  |
|  |  |  |  |
|  |  |  |  |

## DATE

## LOCATION

## GPS

## WEATHER CONDITIONS

## SET-UP

MACHINE & EQUIPMENT

- 

- 

USED SETTINGS

## SKETCHES

## LIST OF ITEMS

| ITEM FOUND | MAIN MATERIAL | WEIGHT & SIZE | VALUE |
|---|---|---|---|
| | | | |
| | | | |
| | | | |
| | | | |
| | | | |
| | | | |
| | | | |
| | | | |
| | | | |
| | | | |

## DATE

## LOCATION

## GPS

## WEATHER CONDITIONS

## SET-UP

**MACHINE & EQUIPMENT**

- 

- 

**USED SETTINGS**

## SKETCHES

## LIST OF ITEMS

| ITEM FOUND | MAIN MATERIAL | WEIGHT & SIZE | VALUE |
|---|---|---|---|
|  |  |  |  |
|  |  |  |  |
|  |  |  |  |
|  |  |  |  |
|  |  |  |  |
|  |  |  |  |
|  |  |  |  |
|  |  |  |  |
|  |  |  |  |
|  |  |  |  |

## DATE

## LOCATION

## GPS

## WEATHER CONDITIONS

## SET-UP

MACHINE & EQUIPMENT

•

•

USED SETTINGS

## SKETCHES

## LIST OF ITEMS

| ITEM FOUND | MAIN MATERIAL | WEIGHT & SIZE | VALUE |
|---|---|---|---|
| | | | |
| | | | |
| | | | |
| | | | |
| | | | |
| | | | |
| | | | |
| | | | |
| | | | |
| | | | |

## DATE

## LOCATION

## GPS

## WEATHER CONDITIONS

## SET-UP

MACHINE & EQUIPMENT

•

•

USED SETTINGS

## SKETCHES

## LIST OF ITEMS

| ITEM FOUND | MAIN MATERIAL | WEIGHT & SIZE | VALUE |
|---|---|---|---|
| | | | |
| | | | |
| | | | |
| | | | |
| | | | |
| | | | |
| | | | |
| | | | |
| | | | |
| | | | |

# DATE

# LOCATION

# GPS

## WEATHER CONDITIONS

## SET-UP

MACHINE & EQUIPMENT

USED SETTINGS

## SKETCHES

## LIST OF ITEMS

| ITEM FOUND | MAIN MATERIAL | WEIGHT & SIZE | VALUE |
|---|---|---|---|
| | | | |
| | | | |
| | | | |
| | | | |
| | | | |
| | | | |
| | | | |
| | | | |
| | | | |
| | | | |

| 📅 DATE | **WEATHER CONDITIONS** | | | | | |
|---|---|---|---|---|---|---|
| 📍 LOCATION | 🌡 —— | ☀️ | ⛅ | 🌧 | ⛈ | ❄️ |
| 🧭 GPS | 🎏 —— | ☐ | ☐ | ☐ | ☐ | ☐ |

## SET-UP

📱 MACHINE & EQUIPMENT

- •
- •

🎚 USED SETTINGS

## SKETCHES

## LIST OF ITEMS

| 💎 ITEM FOUND | 📑 MAIN MATERIAL | ⚖️ WEIGHT & SIZE | 🏷 VALUE |
|---|---|---|---|
| | | | |
| | | | |
| | | | |
| | | | |
| | | | |
| | | | |
| | | | |
| | | | |
| | | | |
| | | | |

## DATE

## LOCATION

## GPS

## WEATHER CONDITIONS

## SET-UP

**MACHINE & EQUIPMENT**

-

-

**USED SETTINGS**

## SKETCHES

## LIST OF ITEMS

| ITEM FOUND | MAIN MATERIAL | WEIGHT & SIZE | VALUE |
|---|---|---|---|
| | | | |
| | | | |
| | | | |
| | | | |
| | | | |
| | | | |
| | | | |
| | | | |
| | | | |
| | | | |

| DATE | WEATHER CONDITIONS |
|------|---------------------|

**DATE**

**LOCATION**

**GPS**

## WEATHER CONDITIONS

🌡 ——    ☀ ⛅ 🌧 ⛈ ❄

🚩 ——    ☐ ☐ ☐ ☐ ☐

## SET-UP

**MACHINE & EQUIPMENT**

•

•

**USED SETTINGS**

## SKETCHES

## LIST OF ITEMS

| ITEM FOUND | MAIN MATERIAL | WEIGHT & SIZE | VALUE |
|------------|---------------|---------------|-------|
|  |  |  |  |
|  |  |  |  |
|  |  |  |  |
|  |  |  |  |
|  |  |  |  |
|  |  |  |  |
|  |  |  |  |
|  |  |  |  |
|  |  |  |  |
|  |  |  |  |

## DATE

## LOCATION

## GPS

## WEATHER CONDITIONS

## SET-UP

**MACHINE & EQUIPMENT**

- 
- 

**USED SETTINGS**

## SKETCHES

## LIST OF ITEMS

| ITEM FOUND | MAIN MATERIAL | WEIGHT & SIZE | VALUE |
|------------|---------------|---------------|-------|
|            |               |               |       |
|            |               |               |       |
|            |               |               |       |
|            |               |               |       |
|            |               |               |       |
|            |               |               |       |
|            |               |               |       |
|            |               |               |       |
|            |               |               |       |
|            |               |               |       |
|            |               |               |       |

| 📅 DATE | | WEATHER CONDITIONS | | | | | |
|---|---|---|---|---|---|---|---|
| 📍 LOCATION | | 🌡 ___ | ☀️ | ⛅ | 🌧 | ⛈ | ❄️ |
| 🧭 GPS | | 🚩 ___ | ☐ | ☐ | ☐ | ☐ | ☐ |

## SET-UP

📟 MACHINE & EQUIPMENT

- 
- 

🎚 USED SETTINGS

## SKETCHES

## LIST OF ITEMS

| 💎 ITEM FOUND | 🗇 MAIN MATERIAL | ⚖️ WEIGHT & SIZE | 🏷 VALUE |
|---|---|---|---|
| | | | |
| | | | |
| | | | |
| | | | |
| | | | |
| | | | |
| | | | |
| | | | |
| | | | |
| | | | |

**DATE**

**LOCATION**

**GPS**

## WEATHER CONDITIONS

| | | | | | | |
|---|---|---|---|---|---|---|
| 🌡 | — | ☀ | ⛅ | 🌧 | ⛈ | ❄ |
| 🎏 | — | ☐ | ☐ | ☐ | ☐ | ☐ |

## SET-UP

MACHINE & EQUIPMENT

USED SETTINGS

## SKETCHES

## LIST OF ITEMS

| ITEM FOUND | MAIN MATERIAL | WEIGHT & SIZE | VALUE |
|---|---|---|---|
| | | | |
| | | | |
| | | | |
| | | | |
| | | | |
| | | | |
| | | | |
| | | | |
| | | | |
| | | | |

| 📅 DATE | WEATHER CONDITIONS |
|---|---|

**DATE**

**LOCATION**

**GPS**

## WEATHER CONDITIONS

☀️ ⛅ 🌧️ ⛈️ ❄️

☐ ☐ ☐ ☐ ☐

## SET-UP

🔋 MACHINE & EQUIPMENT

•

•

🎛️ USED SETTINGS

## SKETCHES

## LIST OF ITEMS

| 💎 ITEM FOUND | 📑 MAIN MATERIAL | ⚖️ WEIGHT & SIZE | 🏷️ VALUE |
|---|---|---|---|
| | | | |
| | | | |
| | | | |
| | | | |
| | | | |
| | | | |
| | | | |
| | | | |
| | | | |
| | | | |

## DATE

## LOCATION

## GPS

## WEATHER CONDITIONS

## SET-UP

MACHINE & EQUIPMENT

•

•

USED SETTINGS

## SKETCHES

## LIST OF ITEMS

| ITEM FOUND | MAIN MATERIAL | WEIGHT & SIZE | VALUE |
|---|---|---|---|
| | | | |
| | | | |
| | | | |
| | | | |
| | | | |
| | | | |
| | | | |
| | | | |
| | | | |

## DATE

## LOCATION

## GPS

## WEATHER CONDITIONS

## SET-UP

**MACHINE & EQUIPMENT**

- 
- 

**USED SETTINGS**

## SKETCHES

## LIST OF ITEMS

| ITEM FOUND | MAIN MATERIAL | WEIGHT & SIZE | VALUE |
|---|---|---|---|
| | | | |
| | | | |
| | | | |
| | | | |
| | | | |
| | | | |
| | | | |
| | | | |
| | | | |
| | | | |

## DATE

## LOCATION

## GPS

## WEATHER CONDITIONS

## SET-UP

**MACHINE & EQUIPMENT**

- 

- 

**USED SETTINGS**

## SKETCHES

## LIST OF ITEMS

| ITEM FOUND | MAIN MATERIAL | WEIGHT & SIZE | VALUE |
|---|---|---|---|
| | | | |
| | | | |
| | | | |
| | | | |
| | | | |
| | | | |
| | | | |
| | | | |
| | | | |
| | | | |
| | | | |

## DATE

## LOCATION

## GPS

## WEATHER CONDITIONS

## SET-UP

**MACHINE & EQUIPMENT**

·

·

**USED SETTINGS**

## SKETCHES

## LIST OF ITEMS

| ITEM FOUND | MAIN MATERIAL | WEIGHT & SIZE | VALUE |
|---|---|---|---|
| | | | |
| | | | |
| | | | |
| | | | |
| | | | |
| | | | |
| | | | |
| | | | |
| | | | |
| | | | |

## DATE

## LOCATION

## GPS

## WEATHER CONDITIONS

## SET-UP

MACHINE & EQUIPMENT

USED SETTINGS

## SKETCHES

## LIST OF ITEMS

| ITEM FOUND | MAIN MATERIAL | WEIGHT & SIZE | VALUE |
|---|---|---|---|
| | | | |
| | | | |
| | | | |
| | | | |
| | | | |
| | | | |
| | | | |
| | | | |
| | | | |
| | | | |

| 📅 DATE | | WEATHER CONDITIONS |
| --- | --- |

| 📅 DATE |
| --- |
| 📍 LOCATION |
| 🧭 GPS |

## WEATHER CONDITIONS

🌡️ ___    ☀️ ⛅ 🌧️ ⛈️ ❄️

🚩 ___    ☐ ☐ ☐ ☐ ☐

## SET-UP

| 📱 MACHINE & EQUIPMENT |
| --- |
| • |
| • |
| 🎚️ USED SETTINGS |
| |
| |
| |
| |

## SKETCHES

## LIST OF ITEMS

| 💎 ITEM FOUND | 📑 MAIN MATERIAL | ⚖️ WEIGHT & SIZE | 🏷️ VALUE |
| --- | --- | --- | --- |
| | | | |
| | | | |
| | | | |
| | | | |
| | | | |
| | | | |
| | | | |
| | | | |
| | | | |
| | | | |

## DATE

## LOCATION

## GPS

## WEATHER CONDITIONS

## SET-UP

**MACHINE & EQUIPMENT**

- 
- 

**USED SETTINGS**

## SKETCHES

## LIST OF ITEMS

| 💎 ITEM FOUND | 🎴 MAIN MATERIAL | ⚖️ WEIGHT & SIZE | 💲 VALUE |
|---|---|---|---|
|  |  |  |  |
|  |  |  |  |
|  |  |  |  |
|  |  |  |  |
|  |  |  |  |
|  |  |  |  |
|  |  |  |  |
|  |  |  |  |
|  |  |  |  |
|  |  |  |  |
|  |  |  |  |

## DATE

## LOCATION

## GPS

## WEATHER CONDITIONS

## SET-UP

**MACHINE & EQUIPMENT**

- 
- 

**USED SETTINGS**

## SKETCHES

## LIST OF ITEMS

| ITEM FOUND | MAIN MATERIAL | WEIGHT & SIZE | VALUE |
|---|---|---|---|
| | | | |
| | | | |
| | | | |
| | | | |
| | | | |
| | | | |
| | | | |
| | | | |
| | | | |
| | | | |

## DATE

## LOCATION

## GPS

## WEATHER CONDITIONS

## SET-UP

MACHINE & EQUIPMENT

- 
- 

USED SETTINGS

## SKETCHES

## LIST OF ITEMS

| ITEM FOUND | MAIN MATERIAL | WEIGHT & SIZE | VALUE |
|---|---|---|---|
|  |  |  |  |
|  |  |  |  |
|  |  |  |  |
|  |  |  |  |
|  |  |  |  |
|  |  |  |  |
|  |  |  |  |
|  |  |  |  |
|  |  |  |  |
|  |  |  |  |
|  |  |  |  |

| 📅 DATE | |
|---|---|
| 📍 LOCATION | |
| 🧭 GPS | |

## WEATHER CONDITIONS

| 🌡 ___ | ☀ | ⛅ | ☁ | ⛈ | ❄ |
|---|---|---|---|---|---|
| 🚩 ___ | ☐ | ☐ | ☐ | ☐ | ☐ |

## SET-UP

| 📱 MACHINE & EQUIPMENT |
|---|
| • |
| • |
| 🎚 USED SETTINGS |
| |
| |
| |

## SKETCHES

## LIST OF ITEMS

| 💎 ITEM FOUND | 🍃 MAIN MATERIAL | ⚖ WEIGHT & SIZE | 🏷 VALUE |
|---|---|---|---|
| | | | |
| | | | |
| | | | |
| | | | |
| | | | |
| | | | |
| | | | |
| | | | |
| | | | |
| | | | |

# DATE

# LOCATION

# GPS

## WEATHER CONDITIONS

## SET-UP

### MACHINE & EQUIPMENT

### USED SETTINGS

## SKETCHES

## LIST OF ITEMS

| ITEM FOUND | MAIN MATERIAL | WEIGHT & SIZE | VALUE |
|---|---|---|---|
| | | | |
| | | | |
| | | | |
| | | | |
| | | | |
| | | | |
| | | | |
| | | | |
| | | | |
| | | | |

| 📅 DATE | | **WEATHER CONDITIONS** |
|---------|---|------------------------|

| 📅 **DATE** |
|-------------|
| 📍 **LOCATION** |
| 🧭 **GPS** |

**WEATHER CONDITIONS**

🌡️ ___  ☀️ ⛅ 🌧️ ⛈️ ❄️

🚩 ___  ☐ ☐ ☐ ☐ ☐

| **SET-UP** |
|------------|
| 📱 MACHINE & EQUIPMENT |
| • |
| • |
| 🎚️ USED SETTINGS |
| |
| |
| |

**SKETCHES**

## LIST OF ITEMS

| 💎 ITEM FOUND | 📑 MAIN MATERIAL | ⚖️ WEIGHT & SIZE | 🏷️ VALUE |
|---------------|------------------|-------------------|-----------|
| | | | |
| | | | |
| | | | |
| | | | |
| | | | |
| | | | |
| | | | |
| | | | |
| | | | |
| | | | |

## DATE

## LOCATION

## GPS

## WEATHER CONDITIONS

## SET-UP

MACHINE & EQUIPMENT

- 
- 

USED SETTINGS

## SKETCHES

## LIST OF ITEMS

| ITEM FOUND | MAIN MATERIAL | WEIGHT & SIZE | VALUE |
| --- | --- | --- | --- |
| | | | |
| | | | |
| | | | |
| | | | |
| | | | |
| | | | |
| | | | |
| | | | |
| | | | |
| | | | |

## DATE

## LOCATION

## GPS

## WEATHER CONDITIONS

## SET-UP

### MACHINE & EQUIPMENT

- 
- 

### USED SETTINGS

## SKETCHES

## LIST OF ITEMS

| ITEM FOUND | MAIN MATERIAL | WEIGHT & SIZE | VALUE |
|---|---|---|---|
| | | | |
| | | | |
| | | | |
| | | | |
| | | | |
| | | | |
| | | | |
| | | | |
| | | | |
| | | | |

## DATE

## LOCATION

## GPS

## WEATHER CONDITIONS

## SET-UP

MACHINE & EQUIPMENT

- 
- 

USED SETTINGS

## SKETCHES

## LIST OF ITEMS

| ITEM FOUND | MAIN MATERIAL | WEIGHT & SIZE | VALUE |
|---|---|---|---|
| | | | |
| | | | |
| | | | |
| | | | |
| | | | |
| | | | |
| | | | |
| | | | |
| | | | |
| | | | |

| 📅 DATE | |
|---|---|
| 📍 LOCATION | |
| 🧭 GPS | |

## WEATHER CONDITIONS

| 🌡 ___ | ☀️ ⛅ 🌧 ⛈ ❄️ |
|---|---|
| 🚩 ___ | ☐ ☐ ☐ ☐ ☐ |

## SET-UP

| 📱 MACHINE & EQUIPMENT |
|---|
| • |
| • |
| 🎚 USED SETTINGS |
| |
| |
| |

## SKETCHES

## LIST OF ITEMS

| 💎 ITEM FOUND | 📚 MAIN MATERIAL | ⚖️ WEIGHT & SIZE | 🏷 VALUE |
|---|---|---|---|
| | | | |
| | | | |
| | | | |
| | | | |
| | | | |
| | | | |
| | | | |
| | | | |
| | | | |
| | | | |

# DATE

# LOCATION

# GPS

## WEATHER CONDITIONS

## SET-UP

MACHINE & EQUIPMENT

USED SETTINGS

## SKETCHES

## LIST OF ITEMS

| ITEM FOUND | MAIN MATERIAL | WEIGHT & SIZE | VALUE |
|---|---|---|---|
|  |  |  |  |
|  |  |  |  |
|  |  |  |  |
|  |  |  |  |
|  |  |  |  |
|  |  |  |  |
|  |  |  |  |
|  |  |  |  |
|  |  |  |  |
|  |  |  |  |

| 📅 DATE | | **WEATHER CONDITIONS** | |
|---|---|---|---|
| 📍 LOCATION | | 🌡 ___ ☀ ⛅ 🌧 ⛈ ❄ | |
| 🧭 GPS | | 🚩 ___ ☐ ☐ ☐ ☐ ☐ | |

## SET-UP

| 📱 MACHINE & EQUIPMENT |
|---|
| • |
| • |
| 🎛 USED SETTINGS |
| |
| |
| |

## SKETCHES

## LIST OF ITEMS

| 💎 ITEM FOUND | 🗂 MAIN MATERIAL | ⚖ WEIGHT & SIZE | 🏷 VALUE |
|---|---|---|---|
| | | | |
| | | | |
| | | | |
| | | | |
| | | | |
| | | | |
| | | | |
| | | | |
| | | | |
| | | | |

## DATE

## LOCATION

## GPS

## WEATHER CONDITIONS

## SET-UP

**MACHINE & EQUIPMENT**

•

•

**USED SETTINGS**

## SKETCHES

## LIST OF ITEMS

| ITEM FOUND | MAIN MATERIAL | WEIGHT & SIZE | VALUE |
|---|---|---|---|
| | | | |
| | | | |
| | | | |
| | | | |
| | | | |
| | | | |
| | | | |
| | | | |
| | | | |
| | | | |
| | | | |

| 📅 DATE | | **WEATHER CONDITIONS** | |
|---|---|---|---|

| 📅 DATE |
|---|
| 📍 LOCATION |
| 🧭 GPS |

| **WEATHER CONDITIONS** |
|---|
| 🌡 ___  ☀ 🌤 ☁ 🌧 ❄ |
| 🚩 ___  ☐ ☐ ☐ ☐ ☐ |

| **SET-UP** |
|---|
| 📟 MACHINE & EQUIPMENT |
| • |
| • |
| ⚙ USED SETTINGS |
| |
| |
| |

**SKETCHES**

**LIST OF ITEMS**

| 💎 ITEM FOUND | 🔶 MAIN MATERIAL | ⚖ WEIGHT & SIZE | 🏷 VALUE |
|---|---|---|---|
| | | | |
| | | | |
| | | | |
| | | | |
| | | | |
| | | | |
| | | | |
| | | | |
| | | | |
| | | | |

## DATE

## LOCATION

## GPS

## WEATHER CONDITIONS

## SET-UP

MACHINE & EQUIPMENT

- 
- 

USED SETTINGS

## SKETCHES

## LIST OF ITEMS

| ITEM FOUND | MAIN MATERIAL | WEIGHT & SIZE | VALUE |
|---|---|---|---|
| | | | |
| | | | |
| | | | |
| | | | |
| | | | |
| | | | |
| | | | |
| | | | |
| | | | |
| | | | |

| 📅 DATE | | **WEATHER CONDITIONS** | | | | | |
|---|---|---|---|---|---|---|---|
| 📍 LOCATION | | 🌡️ ___ | ☀️ | ⛅ | ☁️ | 🌧️ | ⛈️ | ❄️ |
| 🧭 GPS | | 🚩 ___ | ☐ | ☐ | ☐ | ☐ | ☐ |

## SET-UP

🎛️ MACHINE & EQUIPMENT

- 
- 

🎚️ USED SETTINGS

## SKETCHES

## LIST OF ITEMS

| 💎 ITEM FOUND | 📚 MAIN MATERIAL | ⚖️ WEIGHT & SIZE | 🏷️ VALUE |
|---|---|---|---|
| | | | |
| | | | |
| | | | |
| | | | |
| | | | |
| | | | |
| | | | |
| | | | |
| | | | |
| | | | |

## DATE

## LOCATION

## GPS

## WEATHER CONDITIONS

☀ ⛅ 🌧 ⛈ ❄

☐ ☐ ☐ ☐ ☐

## SET-UP

**MACHINE & EQUIPMENT**

**USED SETTINGS**

## SKETCHES

## LIST OF ITEMS

| ITEM FOUND | MAIN MATERIAL | WEIGHT & SIZE | VALUE |
|---|---|---|---|
|  |  |  |  |
|  |  |  |  |
|  |  |  |  |
|  |  |  |  |
|  |  |  |  |
|  |  |  |  |
|  |  |  |  |
|  |  |  |  |
|  |  |  |  |
|  |  |  |  |

| 📅 DATE | |
|---|---|
| 📍 LOCATION | |
| 🧭 GPS | |

## WEATHER CONDITIONS

🌡 ___ ☀ ⛅ 🌧 ⛈ ❄

🚩 ___ ☐ ☐ ☐ ☐ ☐

## SET-UP

| 📱 MACHINE & EQUIPMENT |
|---|
| • |
| • |
| 🎚 USED SETTINGS |
| |
| |
| |

## SKETCHES

## LIST OF ITEMS

| 💎 ITEM FOUND | 🍥 MAIN MATERIAL | ⏱ WEIGHT & SIZE | 🏷 VALUE |
|---|---|---|---|
| | | | |
| | | | |
| | | | |
| | | | |
| | | | |
| | | | |
| | | | |
| | | | |
| | | | |
| | | | |

| 📅 DATE | |
|---|---|
| 📍 LOCATION | |
| 🧭 GPS | |

## WEATHER CONDITIONS

| 🌡️ ___ | ☀️ | ⛅ | 🌧️ | ⛈️ | ❄️ |
|---|---|---|---|---|---|
| 🚩 ___ | ☐ | ☐ | ☐ | ☐ | ☐ |

## SET-UP

🎛️ MACHINE & EQUIPMENT

•

•

🎚️ USED SETTINGS

## SKETCHES

## LIST OF ITEMS

| 💎 ITEM FOUND | 📑 MAIN MATERIAL | ⚖️ WEIGHT & SIZE | 🏷️ VALUE |
|---|---|---|---|
| | | | |
| | | | |
| | | | |
| | | | |
| | | | |
| | | | |
| | | | |
| | | | |
| | | | |
| | | | |

| DATE | WEATHER CONDITIONS |
|---|---|

**DATE**

**LOCATION**

**GPS**

## WEATHER CONDITIONS

| | | ☀ | ⛅ | ☁ | 🌧 | ❄ |
|---|---|---|---|---|---|---|
| 🌡 | ___ | | | | | |
| 🚩 | ___ | ☐ | ☐ | ☐ | ☐ | ☐ |

## SET-UP

**MACHINE & EQUIPMENT**

- 
- 

**USED SETTINGS**

## SKETCHES

## LIST OF ITEMS

| ITEM FOUND | MAIN MATERIAL | WEIGHT & SIZE | VALUE |
|---|---|---|---|
| | | | |
| | | | |
| | | | |
| | | | |
| | | | |
| | | | |
| | | | |
| | | | |
| | | | |
| | | | |

| 📅 DATE | | WEATHER CONDITIONS |
|---|---|---|
| 📍 LOCATION | | 🌡 ___  ☀ ⛅ 🌧 ⛈ ❄ |
| 🧭 GPS | | 🚩 ___  ☐ ☐ ☐ ☐ ☐ |

## SET-UP

📟 MACHINE & EQUIPMENT

· _____

· _____

🎚 USED SETTINGS

_____

_____

_____

## SKETCHES

## LIST OF ITEMS

| 💎 ITEM FOUND | 📚 MAIN MATERIAL | ⚖ WEIGHT & SIZE | 🏷 VALUE |
|---|---|---|---|
| | | | |
| | | | |
| | | | |
| | | | |
| | | | |
| | | | |
| | | | |
| | | | |
| | | | |
| | | | |

| 📅 DATE | | **WEATHER CONDITIONS** | | | | | |
|---|---|---|---|---|---|---|---|
| 📍 LOCATION | | 🌡 ___ | ☀ | ⛅ | 🌧 | ⛈ | ❄ |
| 🧭 GPS | | 🚩 ___ | ☐ | ☐ | ☐ | ☐ | ☐ |

| **SET-UP** | **SKETCHES** |
|---|---|
| 📱 MACHINE & EQUIPMENT | |
| • | |
| • | |
| 🎛 USED SETTINGS | |
| | |
| | |
| | |

## LIST OF ITEMS

| 💎 ITEM FOUND | ⬙ MAIN MATERIAL | ⚖ WEIGHT & SIZE | 🏷 VALUE |
|---|---|---|---|
| | | | |
| | | | |
| | | | |
| | | | |
| | | | |
| | | | |
| | | | |
| | | | |
| | | | |
| | | | |

# DATE

# LOCATION

# GPS

## WEATHER CONDITIONS

## SET-UP

MACHINE & EQUIPMENT

USED SETTINGS

## SKETCHES

## LIST OF ITEMS

| ITEM FOUND | MAIN MATERIAL | WEIGHT & SIZE | VALUE |
|---|---|---|---|
| | | | |
| | | | |
| | | | |
| | | | |
| | | | |
| | | | |
| | | | |
| | | | |
| | | | |
| | | | |

| 📅 DATE | **WEATHER CONDITIONS** | | | | | |
|---|---|---|---|---|---|---|
| 📍 LOCATION | 🌡 ___ | ☀ | ⛅ | ☁ | ⛈ | ❄ |
| 🧭 GPS | 🚩 ___ | ☐ | ☐ | ☐ | ☐ | ☐ |

| **SET-UP** | **SKETCHES** |
|---|---|
| 📱 MACHINE & EQUIPMENT | |
| • | |
| • | |
| 🎚 USED SETTINGS | |
| | |
| | |
| | |

## LIST OF ITEMS

| 💎 ITEM FOUND | 🗐 MAIN MATERIAL | ⚖ WEIGHT & SIZE | 🏷 VALUE |
|---|---|---|---|
| | | | |
| | | | |
| | | | |
| | | | |
| | | | |
| | | | |
| | | | |
| | | | |
| | | | |
| | | | |

## DATE

## LOCATION

## GPS

## WEATHER CONDITIONS

## SET-UP

**MACHINE & EQUIPMENT**

**USED SETTINGS**

## SKETCHES

## LIST OF ITEMS

| ITEM FOUND | MAIN MATERIAL | WEIGHT & SIZE | VALUE |
|---|---|---|---|
| | | | |
| | | | |
| | | | |
| | | | |
| | | | |
| | | | |
| | | | |
| | | | |
| | | | |
| | | | |

## DATE

## LOCATION

## GPS

## WEATHER CONDITIONS

## SET-UP

**MACHINE & EQUIPMENT**

·

·

**USED SETTINGS**

## SKETCHES

## LIST OF ITEMS

| ITEM FOUND | MAIN MATERIAL | WEIGHT & SIZE | VALUE |
|---|---|---|---|
| | | | |
| | | | |
| | | | |
| | | | |
| | | | |
| | | | |
| | | | |
| | | | |
| | | | |
| | | | |

## DATE

## LOCATION

## GPS

## WEATHER CONDITIONS

## SET-UP

### MACHINE & EQUIPMENT

- 
- 

### USED SETTINGS

## SKETCHES

## LIST OF ITEMS

| ITEM FOUND | MAIN MATERIAL | WEIGHT & SIZE | VALUE |
|---|---|---|---|
|  |  |  |  |
|  |  |  |  |
|  |  |  |  |
|  |  |  |  |
|  |  |  |  |
|  |  |  |  |
|  |  |  |  |
|  |  |  |  |
|  |  |  |  |
|  |  |  |  |
|  |  |  |  |

| DATE | WEATHER CONDITIONS | | | | | |
|------|---|---|---|---|---|---|
| LOCATION | — | ☀ | ⛅ | 🌧 | ⛈ | ❄ |
| GPS | — | ☐ | ☐ | ☐ | ☐ | ☐ |

## SET-UP

**MACHINE & EQUIPMENT**

- •
- •

**USED SETTINGS**

## SKETCHES

## LIST OF ITEMS

| 💎 ITEM FOUND | 🔷 MAIN MATERIAL | ⚖ WEIGHT & SIZE | 🏷 VALUE |
|---------------|------------------|-----------------|----------|
| | | | |
| | | | |
| | | | |
| | | | |
| | | | |
| | | | |
| | | | |
| | | | |
| | | | |
| | | | |

Made in United States
North Haven, CT
28 November 2022

27391820R00055